LIVING LIFE

JOSEPH M THOHRII

This book is lovingly dedicated to beloved

Late Mrs. Marie McDermott (1920-2023)

Florida, USA

who generously supported in my formation towards priesthood.

May her soul Rest in Peace.

Contents

Contents

Contents

Contents

Preface

William Wordsworth said *"Poetry is a spontaneous overflow of powerful feelings"*. Human person as we are, we are emotional beings with feelings taking a good control of our rational self. Our feelings are sometimes our expression of our conscious self as well as our unconscious self. Feelings are expressed and sometimes unexpressed. However there are certain times when our feelings are articulated in words and the words may not be the apt one to equate and match our feelings.

The poetries in my book *'Living Life'* are my collections penned during the course of my life's journey from my High school days till my life so far which I believed has been well travelled. The passionate journey of my life has many up's and down's, much more it had rough phases and at times an upheaval climb and a steep roll downward. However with God's grace and blessings, have sailed through for which I remain ever grateful. To my parents who are my foundation and pillar from childhood and given their all in my upbringing and allowed me to become what I am today. To my superiors and companions who always has encouraged and supported me in all my undertakings. To my maternal uncle Shri Henry K Heni IAS (Retired) commissioner, Government of Manipur who willingly agreed to write the Forward of my book. To the young upcoming Entrepreneur RS Zhaipuh Abraham who did the cover illustration with his magnificent art. I am also greatly indebted to Leiyachon Sareo, Assistant Professor, St. Joseph College, Ukhrul for painstakingly and minutely reading through my manuscript and gave a valuable insight for publishing.

Last but not the least, to the publishing house for accepting my work and arranged all the logistic to make my book a reality.

Joseph M Thohrii

Foreword

A society rich in literature reflects a certain well-being and progress of that society. Reflection of the events around us, putting those thoughts into perspective, and putting those thoughts to paper requires a sense of imperative and discipline. We are happy that another volume will soon be released to add to our literature. The author wrote these poems over the course of his life, each poem reflecting his life experiences and perspectives as they evolved over the course of the years. Reading through the author's poems one is taken through the journey of this evolutionary process. While we have different thoughts and perspectives that develop from our own life experiences, it would be valuable to take a glimpse at and understand how a person's life is moulded and shaped by the changes in their thought processes over time.

"Living Life" is a collection of poems by the author, beginning from his younger school days and continuing till date, through the ups and downs of the years. Despite life's inconveniences and difficulties in his journey through life, the author has successfully achieved a career – a priestly life –one he loves so much. It is, indeed, a marvellous achievement! People aspire for much in life but may not always be able to achieve them for some reason or the other. Indeed, life offers us many options and what suits one may not suit another. Fabulously rewarded are the ones who aspire to do certain things in life and then go on to achieve them through sheer single-minded hard work, not worrying too much the noise and distractions that exist around them. The author is one such achiever. I hope the author's tenacious grip of his aim in life, and his dogged determination to overcome the obstacles and struggles to get to where he is now, as

narrated through his poems will be of interest to the reader, and also provide an opportunity for the younger people to reflect upon and may be emulate.

Though our society has yet to produce abundance about our history, tradition, arts and culture, it is heartening to see that our people have started writing books concerning our society. I wish to encourage our people, especially the younger people, to write articles and books through which we can disseminate information about our society to people of other societies and also to our future generations. Much about our society remains unknown to other societies, and perhaps it would not be unfair to say that we ourselves do not have enough knowledge about the old rites and rituals and other finer aspects of life our forefathers practiced. Literature is a treasure house of knowledge, and we would be failing ourselves if we do not pass on enough knowledge of our society to younger generations through the recorded literature.

Henry K Heni IAS (Retd)
Imphal, Manipur

1. I Was Loved by You

When I was down with tears;
and my hopes and dreams shattered,
amidst all troubles and difficulties,
not knowing what further steps to take;
blinded by my sorrows and pains;
asking to whom shall I turn then?
At this time it was you, my dearest,
who touched my heart profoundly
and loved me, strengthened me and
assured your sweet prayers for me daily.
I thank God for the love and
care I experienced through you.
May you ever grow in my heart
and let not time and distance separate us
from the love we had for each other.
I thank God for the prayers and
the love you had given me.

2. Nature's blessing

My dreams and hopes shattered,
discouraged and fed up with my life.
I looked around hoping for something
but nothing seemed to strike me,
as gentle wind blows, the leaves on
the tree around me danced
together with the birds chirping;
makes me delightful and joyful.
The green leaves show freshness,
a strong and a youthful life;
yet amidst the wind joyfully
they dances and are bothered not.
As the wind turns to storm
and the tree with the leaves shook,
to me I felt the tree would collapse,
but not, it shook and stood firm.
And my eyes brightened with hope,
delighted with joy admiring the strength
and calmness of the tree and its leaves,
during the hardships and tranquillity.
I walk'd away learning from them,
as how to endure in life and
face life's challenges with calmness.

3. But Lord, why me?

Thousands of youngsters active,
bright, smart and capable they are,
full of gusto and hope for the future,
never sad but smiling all the way.
Ready to face, 'come what may'
waiting in hope of their future:
young and energetic they look,
Worthy! Even to serve thee Lord,
your given talents and abilities
if harness can best serve you,
and your people, and for your kingdom.
But still you utilise them not
and they not for you, Lord.

But unworthy, sinful and weak,
Intelligent but talented not;
pride, anger and passion rules me,
easy going and life cared not,
like a leaf blown by wind every time
an 'invitation' to serve you .
Why me, and not them? Why me, Lord?
Because…. "I have called you, just and
only you, you are mine," that's it my son.

4. Actually, who am I?

Why thou has sent me here?
To thee I humbly ask now,
in this world; where thou reigns.
Living in fear, and temptation,
cruel face with bitter smile.
To possess and show off always,
pretending to know, whatever be:
trying to outdo others,
critic and gossip, its profession;
humble not, to accept from others,
self-ego and pretention up to
its brim and overflowing.
Yet, still marching towards it
solemnly, to thee whom I've said'
"Yes Lord, here I am your servant".
Not wanting to turn back from thee,
but struggling and fighting to give up,
what all lies within me.
But thou asked me to choose
What all lies within me.
But thou asked me, to choose,
what is in me and what I have;
or to commit and belong to thee alone.
I cried and with bended knee I pray'd,

to show His will and the path to go.
Then confident and firm I stood up,
whispering my last words to Him,
"with generosity and total commitment;
for thee alone and for thy glory"

5. Sweet 19

Gone forever are those days,
Never to come again in this life,
'Sweet teenage years'; seven years;
The memorable diary of one's life.

Gone forever are those days,
But memories still cherish fresh
In one's life, unforgettable they are,
Hope to remain till one's death.

Gone forever are those days,
Experiencing the toughest and the easiest,
Bothered not anything and anywhere,
Making one's life enjoyable always.

Gone forever are those days,
Where one learned and experienced the most
To be a man in the future,
Forget not this age, till eternity.

6. Life's Journey to Eternity

Come and gone are the everyday challenges,
yet they made an impression in my life:
every obstacle making my life change,
giving a new lesson and experience
so as to move towards the final destiny.
Life seem to be an endless journey,
knowing not and aware not when I move
but wanting to reach somewhere call 'nowhere'.
Convinced within, that I should be a man,
and contribute something to this world,
and not just 'come and go' in this world.
The little I know and I have to contribute,
so as when I perish from this sweet land,
the world may remember me by.
Oh! but weak, fearful and talented not,
still with the principle of my life, I stand:
'Be what you are and be at its best'.
and with the plan and aim that,
I should 'Bloom, where I am planted',
so that when I move on to the next world,
on that last judgment day;

the heavenly father who sent me with
a purpose to do His will on earth,
may call me a "Good and faithful servant",
and that should be my final aim.

7. Uncontrollable Anger

Down through my memory lane
recalling how I handle anger;
it is difficult to imagine, yet it is true.
True, surely, but it is indigestible now
never had I conquered with ease,
not even with my whole strength;
in a split of second, come and goes.
Never know the method to tackle
and handle, with it breaking the hearts
of many and even my dignity.
But after these uncontrollable moment,
I regret and weep for what I did,
with bended knees even in the Church,
feeling sorry and with heavy heart bewailed,
'why my action speaks faster than words'.
Asking myself, at that moment:
Where my patience and self-control were?
At last realising, if these two were there,
I could have won many hearts with ease.

8. Humility in Humanity

Humble were men in the ages past,
never had known what pride was,
rational beings but simple they were,
power and arm race in the society
they had never known earlier.
They were simple with high thinking,
creative, not for destruction but
for the growth of entire humanity,
so that the world we live in may
be called 'Home Sweet Home'.

Today, the home is not the same,
changed from bad to worse:
egoistic and selfish now are men,
knowing everything call nothing.
Ignorant and incompetent people
the most in this populous world,
greed and gluttony their profession;
sad and regretful for they have less,
resolving and standing firm
never to sigh and regret again.

Chaos and disorder prevails
but still live some righteous,
never growing tired and weary
of doing good for humanity,
simple living with great vision,
Sweat in their brows but still
striving for a global change,
unheard their names are
giving their life for a better tomorrow:
Great reward awaits you, friends.

9. Cry for Peace

Thousands cry for peace,
ten thousands have they numbered;
from the time of civilization
till date, never have they found.
Organisations and groups formed
only to search and find peace:
the whole world joined together;
as one they search, but in vain.
Some dead and gone before,
in life time never knew about it,
new generation, even worse they are.
Fools this ages are, realised not
that within you lies the 'peace',
never expected there would be
in such corner of the heart.
Peace that can't be bought nor sold,
never can it be exchanged,
but can be given to others
and shared; never too late
to realise, to make a better world.
The channel of peace, I can be to all,

and bring love to the unloved, hope to the hopeless
to make a difference to human history;
that this world be 'peace of land',
instead of being 'piece of land'.

10. Sacrifice of Joy

Living in the twenty first century:
amidst modernity and advancement,
binded with pleasure and passion:
striving for one's comfort alone,
to be alone singly in this world
never even thought of, not even trial,
enjoying to the brim, the one chance
of life which Thou had given us.
But, hail friends, there are few,
unheard and unknown they are to us,
yet praying for you all day and night:
never a day without a prayer for you,
single and alone they are ;
without their spouse and children,
not that they cannot or gave up,
neither incapable or responsible not.
Hail brethren, just to be single;
only all for Him, His master
single they wish to be for Him,
fully aware that by himself cannot,
yet in joy along with Him,
journeying together in this world;
in joy and happiness marching ahead:
hail friend, a joyful sacrifice indeed.

11. You fool, my child!

Happy and joyful are the days,
when I was the first and best:
laughing and merrily proclaiming,
making sure everybody knows,
waiting eagerly for people to say 'Congrats',
tapping myself "you have done it"
and my hard works paid off:
convinced 'I am the best and no one else'.
Never asked God "Why me?" those days,
why I should be the best among others?
Days passed, comes a bright day,
luck favoured not, was I
where I was not the first and best,
but behind few of them, still
not bad was my stand, still good
but discouraged and hopes dashed,
heart grief and tearful eyes,
shy and uncomfortable was me,
for I am not the first and best:
becoming critic of the best,
cursing the one who corrected mine,
angry and giving crocodile smile to many.
But I pray and trusted in Him,
and He gave me the answer:

"When in happy days never had
I asked 'why me'?" And now
In times of tears and sorrows,
I should not ask 'Why me?'."

12. 'Love story of 2001'

Never had I anticipated before
that she would make an impact;
in the little corner of my heart.
O country lass, I hail you,
your smile and beauty tames many,
and I fall victim of your prey.
You know me; and I too, you:
burning in love both;
but both unexpressed by lips
while hearts in romance, both;
never expressed; our love for each other.
Rumours and talks about our love
spoken everywhere in school,
kids and friends fool me,
though confused I am; happy yet
for we know not, but they do;
making our unexpressed love stronger,
chance to last till we die.
But dear, time and situation doesn't,
parted we are till today,
never know where do we exist,
which corner do you live in this world,

neither do I nor you know;
still then, I remember you
even to this day, as the first
casualty in my little heart.

13. 'Romance in 2003'

In a period of stress and storm,
I was a sweet teen; unforgettable era,
impatient to love and to be loved;
uncontrollable passion and zeal,
and finally caught by one in love.
Oh lady! Sweet and full of virtue,
stealing away many hearts
by your mere look and smile;
when you do to me; I'm gone,
lost in the world of romance,
killing me by our beauty.
Aware that many behind you,
but simple and modest you are,
still making all admirers equal.
Gorgeous! to be my future soul mate
was my sole aim, but never revealed,
character and modesty of yours,
will make a good woman.
Rich, will be the gentleman
who wins your heart and life;
proud will be your in-laws;
making a perfect home to live.
But woe! never heard, seen, years gone,
neither letters nor call, not even news:

whispering for you some lines to God,
that what I had hoped to see in you,
from my past experience for the future,
may be the gem for the man;
who'll be your future soul mate.

14. 'Early Winter of 2008'

Full of virtue and grace I was,
almost overflowing, pure in thought,
joyful and happy after refreshed life,
full of missionary zeal and gusto,
'to serve and not to be served'.
marching to a village countryside,
entrusted with responsibilities and duty,
mingling with many people, but
entangled badly only with 'one'.
Like me, single and joyful, she was,
never her looks, smile nor beauty
that charm me, but the quality she possessed
the life she lived, the way she lived.
Marvellous and magnificent they were,
pierced my heart , pricked my conscience,
confused my thought, changed my soul.
Hail, powerful was your life and way;
never had I experienced before till date,
from anyone, not even from a beauty queen.
But great, we dealt ourselves maturely,
controlled emotion and tackled calmly,
never had I regretted our encounter
but came the day we parted,
miles separated us, but

very close in heart and prayers,
never had I realised that you'll
be a nightmare in my dream
and thoughts, spot in my heart.
Inerasable till death, but
for sure will bloom till eternity.

15. Lord, Teach Me How to Pray…

Everyday comes and goes by,
life was a pleasant existence,
no worries and tension about life,
but being born in Christian family:
had certain worries about next life;
forever and eternal, that life would be.
Every morning in prayer I do start,
and in prayer do I end the day;
punctual and regular in prayers,
never failing and still keeping up.
Sometimes, dreaming or dozing away
when I don't pray but they were unintentional;
never had I such a desire even,
but what do I pray for?
Neither a prayer of Thanksgiving,
not even for strength nor repentance,
not even for wealth nor fame;
never had I recalled after prayer,
What really did I pray for?
At times confused and irritated
with my life; as a chosen one,
worried for I am to be…..
Another Christ, light to His people,

His messenger on earth, and;
Woe! I've to bring people closer to him,
when I am not close to him.
Lord, teach me how to pray…,
for with 'you' in prayer, I can
do marvels, wonders and greatness
for 'you' and for 'your glory'.

16. A Life That Will Be Forever....

Only one chance to live on this earth;
not even twice; not even by chance,
knew not how long it will be,
destined by fate; cannot presume even,
everyday seems to be the end,
could never even think about it,
for doubt and fear comes at once.
But me! I have a plan to live this life,
for the one who had given me
this chance to live this life.
Long or short may be my life
But only and all for Him alone...

17. Plan to be….

What lies ahead of me?
Where does my next step fall?
Never do I know where I'll be:
in the next moment of life.
Unprepared and fear to face life,
challenges and hurdles awaits,
but lacking trust and confidence,
neither do I have vision for future.
But easy, life would be, if 'planned',
for 'no man plan to fail; but fail to plan'
hard but true are the words.
Awake! realise it, never too late;
for you to plan for the future.

18. Old and Young Heart

The two met in foreign land;
in early autumn; years ago,
Both unknown to each other,
never seen before; but fate alone.
At the first sight smiled when they met,
never had realised or hoped that their
hearts would yearn for each other:
for age was their difference as;
sister old and brother young.

Months they stayed together on duty,
during which they discern their love
was really true, doubtless now:
for they confirmed their 'true love'.
Slowly warmed up their hearts
and enjoyed their holidays.
But destined to part one day,
and now comes; he leaves her
for his duty days over.

But keeping in touch both, through:
letters and people; risky but
'No fear as they are true lovers'.
Great friend, you won the hearts

of million; who are unloved.
proved the world that age doesn't
really matter for true lovers;
'Old in age but young in heart'.
was your dearest sister, that's
what you taught me my friend.

19. Life Rule by Pride

Everyday life seems happy and joyful;
life seems to be without sorrow:
come and gone are every day's tasks
faced with courage and confidence,
never had I realised that it was 'He"
who gave me strength to overcome.
I thought 'I' was the one who did everything;
and by myself made me what I am;
I failed to give gratitude to the one,
who made it possible for me.
Now, angry and frustrated I am,
regretted and wept for my deeds.
But again it was 'He' who came,
'to console me and make me strong',
comforted and made my life new,
after this marvels and wonders,
he had worked in my life:
difference seen in the joy and
happiness which I had before.

20. Silence

Surrounded all around by noise,
endless voices echo in my mind;
never had I experienced the
golden moments of silence:
rarely found, hardly heard now
but doesn't mean it's not there.
To realise the power of silence ,
to realise the depth of silence,
truly difficult to imagine it;
desired long for this beauty,
marvellous it would be,
when I possess it; and for
years I would always cherish.

21. A Moment to Remember

With smiles we live together there,
joys and sorrows we shared,
laughed and wept together,
shared our hearts' feelings;
in eagerness and enthusiasm listened,
every word carries meaning,
mind and thoughts can't grasp,
only after contemplation we can.
Painful was the moment we parted,
in tears I journeyed back home,
to where I'm destined to reach.
Memories always haunted me
and her image always before me,
sleepless nights I underwent for days.
Her angelic words reflect my mind
never easy to erase it away,
especially her beautiful smile which
shows the purity of her heart and soul.
Oh dear! how I longed to see
and hear from you; can be only
a look or even a word;
a year feels like thousand years
but those moments with you are
like eternity in heaven's glory.

22. The Best of All

Born of the same line of race,
like anyone of us; born together,
dedicated and served all with love
happiness and smiles to all;
shared the mother's responsibilities,
lighten the mother's burden,
joyful and showed no anger:
gentle and modest her life,
sacrificed, for love her spirit,
cared and nurtured siblings:
revered and respected elders,
and feared God alone.
But early was the call received,
to be with the Master,
for faithfully you served the world.
and now for the master only
till eternity; and you first
because 'He' saw that you're
among us 'The Best of All'.

23. Childhood Fears

In fear and with it I grew up
Cry and shout when left alone,
fear of dark, death and so forth
whispers of horrors listened;
Curious and questions how,
but at night sleepless for fear.
With this I grew up and
even today all this haunt me
still fresh as childhood days,
but slowly erased away now
for all these seem nothing:
except one, above everything which
I never realised was to know fear
that is only 'fear of God'.

24. Death

Ages had passed, and more yet to come
man had come and gone,
and whoever comes, faces death.
Great or small all bowed to it;
mighty warriors, defeated by death,
kings, rulers, all mercilessly defeated.
Landlord and slaves, everyone
where justice is being shown,
Some reluctant but compelled,
some early and some late,
some fast and some slowly,
some in fear and some courageously,
some in sadness and some joyfully.
But everyone have to face,
the day and hour not fixed,
any moment and anywhere;
Be prepared, for what really
matter is : 'How you face death?'

25. A Blue Night Remembered

Miles away from me up above,
yet clear and beautiful to see,
the moon brightly shines and
the stars dancing in delight:
twinkling all the way;
the heavenly bodies move about,
everything above gives joy and
thrills our life here below.
Gazing at these marvels and wonders,
made me to recall and remember:
the night and time once spent
with family and friends,
sweet, cheerful and memorable days,
happy and laughing whole heartedly:
worries and sadness never thought of,
never realised that I would be left alone;
uncalled and unheard today.
Days to come seem not the same,
for the life I have chosen seems
different from others:
sacrifice and commitment its priority.
But oh! beautiful blue night,
cherished memories you brought

and unforgettable life's events;
gave me the thought that I'm
with them and one beside them:
even though in reality miles away.

26. Fresh and Dry Moments

A day begins with light;
ends with darkness covered,
between beginning and end;
lies a long period of day,
may be sunny or rainy weather
bright or gloomy atmosphere;
and this makes one's life,
fresh and dry moments;
Everyone faces both moments:
ought and compelled to face,
spares none from this dice,
at times joyful to the zenith;
and at times painful to the core,
but this is what makes life,
and makes life worth living.

27. Not Profession but Vocation

Thousands had come and gone,
they came, saw and went away.
Very few came and persevered
they knew it won't be an easy one
for they foresaw the battle ahead;
tough and challenging it would be
but it doesn't mean it is impossible
for it is Christ himself
who leads and guides the path.
And to those who run the race,
complete the battle, and whose
seeds died off; learned that:
alone by oneself could do nothing,
for it wasn't a career or profession
but a vocation; a call received;
which, indeed is given only to few.

28. Journey Home

Hundreds of roads leading home,
all seem good and enjoyable.
Different and unique they all are;
challenges and hardships vary
depends on how one handles.
Time, days and years given;
to decide which one likes,
as not to regret in the days to come;
if taken another road....
the sadness which will come,
the tragedy which may occur
for your hasty decision:
can never be compromised,
and the joy and happiness
which you are likely to get,
if made a right decision
will be lost for eternity.

29. Joy in Sharing

Born not to be alone,
but as a family we live
encountering many experiences
sometimes sweet and at other times bitter,
when sweet in joy we laugh,
when bitter in pain we mourn:
everyone experiencing everything.
The joys when shared multiply
enlighten the hearts and souls,
and the pain when shared divides,
each in its heart the tears
but when shared among all are reduced,
and gives life, hope and love to all,
and in joyful tears we bear;
and march as one heart and soul.

30. Await in Hope

Blessed and great was this day
not for all but for me alone;
Celebrating with hope and joy
cherishing old sweet memories
for miles set us apart
but in thought and prayer close.
Unfortunate and luck favoured not
for we weren't destined to be together
not fortunate even to call you,
to wish you; on this day of yours,
for I am kept on watched.
Oh! I know not, where you are
unheard from you for a year,
not even your voice nor letters
your promise seem unfulfilled
never more to be fulfilled,
Waited in vain for you,
before this day to reach,
not even a sign oh! dear.
But my hope in you remains still
even till my last breath
for my promise to you was
with commitment and trust,
never had I made such a thing

to a human person; except God,
Oh dear! You seem to have forgotten
that such was our promise,
but still in hope do I wait,
never will I break this vow
even if you remember me not.

31. Mummy I love you!

Deep down I always ask myself
"Who love me the most on earth here?",
asking everyone I met and encountered,
travelled wide and researches made,
thought about it far and wide,
reflected and meditated upon.
Always thought someone special
and great may that person be,
somewhere and when I'll meet
was always a dream.
But none other, I was surprised
to know the truth, that you are,
simple and gentle, loving and caring
full of virtue and grace,
joyfully and happily nurtured me,
with great hope and confidence raised me,
and you are the greatest woman,
ever lived in my time and era,
it was none other than you
Mom and only you will be;
I love you forever, Mummy.

32. Manipur, Cry For Peace

A beautiful land, one called:
'Jewel of India' and 'Switzerland of India',
by a great man who once lived.
Peaceful and lovable place it was once.
People flock to see the land
Rich and beautiful cultural heritage
but now people in group flee away
feared and risky even to live now.
Cry our people for peace!
never give up till we get for,
our land must be called and
be known as a land of peace.

33. Burning Manipur

The land where I grew up
and where I ought to die,
for where I receive much,
and where in return I ought to give,
happy, joyful and enjoyable to live in
hard and painful to leave; for duty demands.
Thought I will be back soon
but now sad and afraid to come back
for killing and bloodshed never end,
feels like anytime I may die,
this thought saddened me much
and always and forever will pray that
this land which I once lived and grew up in
may not be burned away.

34. Live Life's Beauty

Every day, it's a new day
every life of every one is different,
every day we journey in life
everyone with a different route,
in our journey we fail and succeed,
in tears and sorrows we meet failure
and in joy and smile we embrace success.
A mixture of joy and sorrow;
a combination of smiles and tears
together multiplies life's beauty.

35. Ode to Dodo

Oh Dodo! the bird once sang on earth
chanted the songs of the wonders
soared high and dazzled the skies,
enthralled the whole atmosphere on earth
grifilled the light of the world.
Oh Dodo! Beauty and hope surrounds,
spreaded fragrance of peace and love,
comforted the refugees and homeless,
consoled the weary travellers
yet in their hands you fell,
their greed, so cruel and indifferent.
Oh Dodo! hail dodo, the world
would never see thee anymore,
never again oh Dodo! forever.

36. Dilemma in the Call

Thou has given me a great desire
to follow you and imitate you,
to be another Christ, 'here I am';
sinful and unworthy as I am.
Now comes the dilemma in the call,
for all seems best and none better;
I say 'here' but they say 'there',
some pressurises to join from where
they have come about and what they are.
This haunted me day and night,
the inner peace was never found,
the conflict within me continues,
the search for vocation within my vocation
the never ending search continues,
and seems like it will continue forever.
I prayed, reflected and took courage
whatever and wherever I may be,
I am going to be a 'priest of God',
for the universal Church and not anybody.

37. Joyous Joy

The joy that we receive unfold
flowing abundantly from thy hand
in abundance he pour upon us
careless and unknown we receive
good and bad he give to us all,
but now depends on us how we use
and how we share among us.

38. Living by flesh

Years and ages gone by,
the battle with flesh remains;
the joy the flesh gives
and more so the pleasure received
remains inexpressible at that time.

The pain it takes to give up,
the sorrow I bore for my sins,
the gravity of the sins increased
made me panic for it but
still had to give up the pleasure.

The joy when I gave up yet
more joyous when I gave in;
and regret thereafter till I resolve
but becomes prey to his pleasure.

Where the strength to overcome lies?
It is 'Thou", O Lord who gav'th me.

39. Burning Desire

Burned up by desire for pleasure,
Pleasure of unending satisfaction,
desire to gratify the senses;
sense of touch, feel and hear,
never ending desire seeming to be.
Pained much to avoid the occasion,
Willed and intended that very moment:
fulfilled and satisfied was the passion
gratified to the full; yet never satisfied:
never thought it was sinful that moment.

40. Await in Glory

Gently and swiftly time passed by,
hours today, days to months and years,
never seem to be on track with her,
though painful, seemed she'd forgotten.
In thought always, but never in dream,
my prayers unheard, gone with the wind.
The news that she remembers, would delight
my soul, and I await in glory for that.

41. A Journey Set to Begin

As I travel life's beautiful passage
a journey to the undestined end;
joys and sorrows accompanied me,
laughter and tears followed me.
Every day's a new day, and so every night
every challenge handled with a difference
every anger made to pass in silence
and every smile shared to all.
Friends and colleagues all not the same,
some supports, some discourages
many at times gossips till it pains
but such was life's endeavour.
The clear conscience makes me feel good,
happy with the contributions I've made
and never to be regretted upon them;
Brought joy and smile in the life and
hearts of many who journey along.

42. Tears of Love

The journey of both the spouses,
from the day they share their vows;
the road seems always not good
sometimes deep ditches and heavy jolts.
To stick to the destiny and carry on,
endure the trials and patiently run
also in tears one weeps for the beloved
at times even depart and separate
but promise for eternal love promised sworn;
for love needs sacrifice in tears.

43. The Child's Cry

Mama's child cries for life
to be one among every child,
but laughter and joy seems denied
and the monster of darkness cover'd .
The chance to life looks bleak
and this seems to be the child's fate,
predestined to face human's cruelty
and missed to see the light of the world.
The unborn child's cry to be given a chance;
to grow up like any other child.

44. The Joy of Every Day

Every day comes and goes by
to some doesn't make any difference
life seems boring and passes by
making no impact upon us and others.
To make any day a special difference
we set out a different journey,
every one's journey the same
but the journey taken differently
makes the everyday living joyful;
this is the purpose of living and
the celebration of being alive.

45. I Believe

I believe that I am what I can become.
I believe that I can make a change.
I believe that I can make a difference.
I believe that I can be a blessing to all.
I believe that I can bring love to many.
I believe that I can be a channel of peace.
I believe that I can be more humane to others.
I believe in the optimistic way of life.
I believe in the realistic approach to life.
Above all I believe in what I belief

46. God of our ancestors

Generations have passed yet you alone are our God.
Down the ages till today you are our everything.
Even though we are sinners, yet you made us worthy;
worthy to worship you; made worthy to be in your presence.
You did not count our failure, neither keep record of our sins
yet you love us; the love that is unconditional.
In our worry you did not dishearten us but strengthened us,
in our sorrows you did not forget us but consoled us,
in our happiness you did not leave us but cheered us,
in our dryness you did not abandon us but enlightened us
in our everything you are there beside us, behind us and above us.

47. Lord, Show Me...

Lord, show me the way I should go
the state that I should belong
the way of life you've planned for me
so that I may serve you faithfully
and be counted as worthy in your kingdom.
Lord before you formed me,
you know me and had a plan for me
a plan that will bring hope and
light to the world and the entire humanity
and not destruction and condemnation.
Lord you know my weakness and falling
my failure and my shortcoming,
in this trials and temptations of my life
strengthen me and give enormous courage
that I may be a joyful victor to these sins.
Lord, you know my needs even before I ask
you know my heart even before I open to you.
Come within me and take control of me
so that when I possess you; you will
be the power and force of my life.
Lord, you stand tall in my life
even though I am a sinner, a deliberate one
yet you do not count on my unworthiness

but loved me with a love that is unconditional beyond measure so that
I may love you more. Lord, you remembered me even when I don't,
you searched me even when I go astray,
and brought me back where I am now.
Such is your love and guidance for me,
so lord, if you will, make me worthy to follow you.

48. Prepare Me, O Lord

Prepare me, O Lord, to be your witness,
to radiate you to the ends of the earth,
but first, make me worthy to give
and carry you, cleanse me
and my lips so that I may proclaim you
and your word worthily,
worthy not in human eyes, but in yours.
Make me pure and holy as you are
and make of me a visible sign
of your presence amidst humankind.
Touch me so that I may be transformed,
love me so that I may know you better,
and most of all make me like you.

49. The 'Yes' for Eternity

The soft whisper, 'Yes' in my prayer;
in an unconscious state of mind,
never thought it would be so powerful,
never imagined it would carry a meaning.

At times doubt hovers over the mind
struggles and hardships take over
giving a thought to the green pasture of life
the 'No' seems to outshine the 'Yes'.

The fight and inner conflict continues
the supremacy of which one was discerned,
and the first soft whisper of 'Yes' stands high,
no turning back and the 'Yes' for eternity remains.

50. Power of Silence

Calm and serene moment of life
when everything around in control
even nature seems at one with;
the chirping birds' voices melodious
join the chorus with the angels;
the cold breeze dances the leaves'
the green around enliven the earth,
vibrant and active the small creature,
the human mind seems at ease
recharging the energy within him
never feel wearied with what is
joyful and cheerful with this look.
The serenity of silence preserved by few
had in abundance benefited the humanity.

51. Just to say 'I Remember You'

Every day I think and dream about you
every time I feel we are in eternity
every night I whisper a prayer for you
every star which illumine the sky;
made me remind of your smile
which had brightened my dark life.
Every thought we share enlighten our mind
every laughter we share dispels our sorrow
every tears we share wipe away our pains
every glance we share, feels we are together
every work we do lighten each other's burden
every single step I take leads towards you
for all these I'm grateful to you and
called up, just to say, 'I Remember You'.

52. You've Touched Me, and I've Grown

When I was only a seedling tiny and small
you watered, nurtured and nourished me;
shy, frightful and pushy I was,
never thought that I'll be what I am today;
little did I know about you
never realised how great you'll be to me;
immeasurable your life had inspired me,
uncountable that you're a blessing to me,
meticulously you car'd for my life
you didn't want me to lose sight of what I'll be,
you were always there beside me and by me to lead,
like a guiding star from above,
a guardian angel for my weary soul.
Oh! dear, how much I'm indebted to you
how can I repay your marvellous deeds?
My gratitude and humble prayers are only a half
to what you had done for my life
my love for you will only be temporary
yet what you desire and want me to be,

is what I can do;
that will be the complete fullness
you have loved me much, cared and inspired me;
you've touched me and I've grown.

53. Days and Life

Come and gone are the sweet days
never to come back again;
passes away like the cool breeze,
chilled the place and blown away,
so also is life's wonderful existence
come and gone like a split of second.
Life's adventurous journey quickly passes,
without any envy and regret live life;
life's struggles ought to be faced with courage
life's joys ought to be shared every day
every moment ought to be lived to the fullest.

54. Jewels of life

The jewel of life: our parents,
the giver of everything on earth,
the visible god they are here,
through whom we know God better.
They are the pearl to every child;
they are God's greatest blessings to every child;
learned or unlearned they may be
yet divine wisdom flow from them.
Our life today is what they did,
to make every child the best they strive.
Boundless and endless sacrifice rendered
that we may be a joy to them.
When we become someone in future,
all their labour and sacrifice vanished
joyful and happy to see that you've made them
proud till grave in smile they lay cherished.

55. Priest; Another Christ

A wretch call to serve Christ;
to share in the priesthood of Christ,
unworthy and unholy as anyone,
weak and sinful yet he hear the call;
now transformed, to live by the call,
to live the life He chose him to live.
Ready to give up one's hardest passion,
sacrifice the joy of married life forever,
in Him he trust, takes up joyful celibacy;
together with, obey the will of his master,
the authority in obedience we live a life,
a life ready to give up even the things:
material possessions, good they may serve
yet may hamper, to lead and know Him.
The cost to serve for His kingdom demanded;
commitment and faithfulness to the call,
hard and painful but moving forward for a purpose,
this is what the first 'yes' cost you.

56. Power of Words

The beauty of powerful words,
so strong that pierce human hearts;
transform, change and enliven souls,
words though casual yet meant.
With gratefulness and sincerity in heart,
'Thank You' we say in love;
when hurt and anger ruled;
whisper in regret 'I'm sorry'.

And in request seek for strength;
calmly and gently ask 'please'.

57. A Home Away from Home

58. Tarnish the Rusted Mortal

Never thought life was to make a turn
a young rascal who looked rusty;
in mind and heart already conceived
never again would be made anew;
life's journey seems all well
but needed badly a thorough refinement.

Never can anyone transform so;
also can by himself at all,
neither an angel takes its place
and hope was all dashed and scattered
then came the rays of hope;
a ray that illumine the dark world.

And this, has made life fascinating,
unthinkable and unimaginable. Now,
that what one has chosen should one stick
confusion and life's dilemma continue
what I ought to be and ought to become,
but still that ray of light strengthens the 'yes'.

59. How I Miss…

How I Miss… to miss you, Miss,
a nightmare in my dream and life,
your smile pierced my soul and
your words shook my firm decision.
You made me to rethink the life I live,
encouraged and boosted my ability,
that I will be a better person, the other way.
Life's opportunities you showed me
and elevated me to the brim, even overflowed
to show me another way of life
which is likely to suit me.
Your smile stole my heart's desire,
melted partly the cream of my life;
miserably left me in a cold unknown world
where life was kept wandering.
Now to erase your footprint in my life,
is just unthinkable and seems impossible,
wondered whether our togetherness is a
'blessing in disguise' or either
a chance to make real life's decision.

60. A fool for Thy kingdom

Life is not what I think should be,
not even what they think I must be,
nor not even what the world want me to be
but what He has destined me to be.

Life can hold me good I decided,
they thought I would be even better,
the world felt I would be a perfect family man,
but instead He chose me to serve them all.

Life, I feel was all what I am
they feel I won't manage this life,
the world feels all is not well,
but He assures me that 'all is well'.

Life, thought would be easy and sober,
they thought it would be miserable,
the world thought it would be boring;
but He foretells it will be a challenge.

Life, I presume would end with death,
they presume it would be difficult,
the world presumes it would be as usual,

but He promises heaven's eternal reward.

Life, I hope can be managed singly
they hope it would be lonely;
the world hope to see life's uniformity
but He would be everything for me, I hope.

61. A Homeward Journey

I took a homeward journey
to return to where I started.
I decided to come back where I began,
unfurled and unfinished the race
an incomplete battle which I fought.
I feel I'm running the wrong track,
determined that I'm off track,
thought I will stumble and fall;
before being too late, I thought
I will surrender the lone battle.
Weak and single handedly defending
without guide and a helping hand,
a lone runner and fighter of the age,
never knew generations would ever remember
in hope awaits the destined destination.

62. Return of the Would Be

The last hope of the generation is gone,
the battle is left unfinished;
to finish the journey only halfway
on the way to whisper the final end
to tell the generations to talk about,
that the journey taken was only half done.
Enlighten me with wisdom to pronounce your life
a single word to know the state of life,
just simple but it meant everything.
Rethink! to face life's reality,
to see the long cherished childhood dream,
to make the early memoirs a destination;
just to tell the world, ' I lived my dream',
and it was worth living and worth dying for.

63. Just to Say…

I was born just to say I once lived.
I was smart just to say I was second to none.
I was handsome just to say I attracted many.
I was aggressive just to say I ruled over others.
I was fast just to say I was never slow.
I was good just to say I was the best.
I was greedy just to say I have ample.
I was selfish just to say I have abundant.
I was possessive just to say I was wealthy.
I was brave just to say I was fearless.
and now I say I've lived just to say.
I could not conquer death.

64. Do You Remember

Do you remember that we grew up together?
How we fac'd the same sunshine,
splashed by the same rain and water,
shared joy and happiness with each other,
wiped each other's tears and shared pain,
smiling and cheering each other always
never was an obstacle to each other
but always a hope and strength.
But fate was what determined our life,
in this world, never will we be one,
for the way of the world demands;
selfish and egoistic feeling of oneself.
Dear! on this earth we'll separate
for a timely parting of young hearts
but to be eternally united in the next,
as one, never to be separated again
and our true love will remain eternal.

65. But the Father's Love

Bewilder'd and cast away life,
lavish and cosy life spent away,
now nothing left, where to head to
but convinced of a welcoming heart
that I would be received as a son again.
The father waiting in hope for his son
to return, to come back home,
the one flesh and blood met
forgiving heart and never ending love
that's the father's love one treasures.

66. The Way That I am

Long have I journeyed in life's race,
carrying along with me life's experiences,
sweet moments always to be cherished
hard moments teach valuable lessons,
smiles and laughter's change hearts,
tears, pains made me stay tough.
Gone are the soft days of life
where emotions and feelings were in control,
pretending to win hearts are the time:
new challenge's experiences win hearts,
became master of life and handled chaos
with prudence and sincere heart,
fighting for truth and living by it to die
for 'called' to be the "Truth" on earth.

67. Prick me not, my conscience

Torture and detest me not, dear conscience
I am dumb and motionless
unable to reason and think
make me know the way I should do.
Teach me the things I should do
how and when to do as I don't.
Make me clear of what I should do,
wisdom to speak at that time;
and prudence to act at that moment,
that I may become what I should be.

68. Do I have to suffer for you?

As I journey along life's highway,
swiftly striding on the crossroad path,
meeting you lightens my life and heart,
a wonderful journey of life awaits
where two souls would be one forever.
But never did I know that barriers
would follow us through and through,
never to leave as we take our untrodden path.
The distance and gap ache our hearts, made
worse the life of yearning souls,
weary the quest for life becomes.
I rise to see what people do not see,
to begin how they never began,
to live just the way others never had,
to love as never been loved before,
for I'm sure 'All is well' with me,
and this will definitely lead me
to end well forever with you.

69. Those Village Days…

The bygone days of the sweet big village
placed on the hills and vales across
fresh and lively are the greens of the land;
smiles and joys always surround the people
greeting with love, for you came to give;
not to take and forever my life be theirs.
with this began the journey of a thousand miles,
to plough and till the land which I ought to,
never to look back to where I started,
not peeping at the other side of the land;
but to work for the promise land in these hills:
begotten village and living faith of the people.
A year gone by I look and smile just,
marvellous were His hands upon thy servant,
now to say 'Thank you' and 'Goodbye'
unimaginable was the journey with you all, tears
of joys roll, memories cherished for
a simple path but a wonderful journey.

70. The bird Next to My Window

The chirping bird who live next to me,
my sweet day begin with your song;
make me eager to see the new day,
with vigour and enthuse for the day,
singing the sweet melancholy of life.
You chirp my life in a better note,
tune my life with the energy I deserved,
module my strength in the proper channel ring
in my ear with good thoughts;
strike my mind with great zeal
to start with hope, end in fulfilment
that's how you, dear marvellous sparrow,
you teach me every day to start anew,
and begin my life daily in the right note.

71. I believe the way you believed

Just the way you believe me, I believed you;
just the way you trusted me, I trusted you;
just the way you smile at me, I smiled at you;
just the way you are to me, I am to you.
We rolled our lives together the way we are,
never wanted to see you sad and cry.
I whisper a mournful ballad in pain
that you and I share a string of souls,
for I cannot but love you, love to death.
the hungry souls of two young heartthrobs,
never a blink in my mind without you,
just the way you love me, I love you, dear.

72. Glimpse of My Dream

Sweet was the glimpse of my dream,
last lonely night in a cold land
fussed where to go and land
couldn't imagine it was 'you'.
The angel of my fabulous night,
short yet was happy with you,
seeming never to be sad a moment;
a reality of love in a reel world.
Fair lady, true was our love and pure,
not a trace of dirt nor lie;
genuine and immortal bond of unity.
the seasons dances with our true love,
Angels rejoice to feel our togetherness;
Heaven awaits our eternal matrimony;
the "I do" of two pure lovely souls.
the dream dar'd to come true ever,
salutes our 'True' and 'Immortal' love,
Lady love, heaven awaits our 'union',
to see us as 'one', even we be 'two'.

73. Wildest dream

Sweet as honey was the kiss eternal,
Soft and tender, the magnificent face;
Chilly and cold the night was
But you warmth my heart and life.

Gratified the souls of two young lovers
Never had we felt such power of love;
Promised love of the committed souls,
But, the kiss enliven my life forever.

74. Heart that Love

The heart that never lov'th before;
given not to anyone, was my love before;
untold to the world, was my love story;
but awaiting for a consecrated divine love.
Came into my life a pure unblemished soul
consecrated for a divine love with me
that taught me to love and be loved.
Hail! gentle queen that throbbed my heart,
burns the unchaste love of my being
smear'd my soul with pure divine love.
Oh! Fair lady to a passionate soul;
wrap me in your bosom to belong to you
that force never can separate our divine love.
Dear sweet eternal lover and virgin pure, not
even in death do us part and unloved; divine,
eternal will my love be for you.

75. Sleep! Thou shalt I Conquer

Thou oh! sleep, you behest me every day;
Night and day you haunted me,
morning's best hours you steal away;
cruel and without mercy you salvage
my sweet moment to be in His presence;
unable to experience the touch of the divine.
call me to be with you when silence dawn, take
me till I remember not what is around me
but help me taste the honey of the divinity,
with peace in the silence of prayer,
that I may be counted worthy of Him,
as I serve Him for all eternity.

76. Wonder for eternity

77. City of Joy

As I walk the lanes of the 'city of Joy',
a city filled with vigour and enthusiasm,
spirit and life, above all sweetness all around.
A city once I longed to step in,
a place where history once beaconed.
the land which brought India to reality.
Hail! The soil that produce legends,
Harken not to few who spoil the image; but
live to carry the country that we love. Never did
the irony of life leave the city, where two
opposing contrasts of life live,
the horror and night-mares do exist here.
A city of multiple skyscrapers and buildings,
yet multiple beggars and rags dwell,
a home where hundreds of full belly people laugh,
yet a refuge of thousand empty stomachs cry,
salute still the city of spices sand mixture,
a land of despair for few;
but a city of hope for many and
that is what the 'City of Joy' is about.

78. Could I smile like before?

A true gentle smile which I once possessed,
a pure smile that stole hearts,
a smile that moved people to tears,
gone and perished are those instinct.
The virginal smile that penetrates life's hurdles,
the glimpse that melts genuine souls,
the look that pulls the solitary life,
whatever be, that smile is gone forever,
hard to get back and wear again,
the smile that won pure gentle souls.
Gone away, faded away and lost forever,
never for eternity to put on,
that which since the day I was born
gifted to me, to give new life to humanity.

79. The Fear of Old Age

The clock of life ticks every moment,
never it has stopped to wait for,
every single moment it rushes fast,
to tell the young that you are ageing.
As you become aged, today's world ditch you,
the son whom you nursed leaves you,
the son whom you hoped for,
ditches you, abandons you and is gone.
The son who brought joy to your life once,
brought today tears as you take leave, the
promised son broke your heart,
left you in a cruel lonely world.
Gone with the time the yesteryears
the smile never to come again
forever thinking of the son that is away, hoping
that he would see them off.

80. The Await of End

Long have I longed to see the end,
the end that close the chapter,
the solace in a little convenience
and take deep sigh of pleasure.
The inning that seems endless,
the day that seems years,
the minutes that seems stopped,
and the world around looks dead.
Whatever be the end is clear;
to see the dawn of a new life.

81. Doubt the Pure Soul

I am in love, that first sight,
the thought of her danced in,
day in and day out sometimes
from months to years it pass'd,
that very first sight caught me.
For years unheard and unseen,
know not where dwell the soul
but her thought twinkles at times;
and a string of joy passes me,
an unexpected smile waves by
when I hear your synonymous name.
Admit do I that remember you
not every day nor every moment
but within me and in my heart
you lie hidden, but not erupted,
to find you that you too love me.
Sweet gentle soul, I found you as you are
just that person whom I have a crush on
who once brought smile and cheers me,
whom once I could not express love
but now you are the life I am.
Ages didn't diminish our love and commitment,
neither can barriers and doubt assail us,
remember we just are meant for eternity.

82. Your Name and Time

The name that rings my mind,
the name that pricks my heart,
the name that tickle, my soul,
that five letter which changed my life.
The time that set us apart,
the time that divided our hearts
the time that multiplied our joys
that five years which happened, happens.
But that five letter that have power,
that five years that taught me lessons,
the five months now we are in
the five days that make us long
the five hours that we share
the five minutes that we decide
the five seconds that can say 'I love you"
so that the new five letter is
renewed and transformed to new life
and the five letter word 'marry' not now
but 'me' who prepare to give,
the best, purest and the genuine
gift that for ages have prepared.

83. The Weary Soul

The soul once pure and holy
the soul once seek the almighty,
the supreme, the source of life.
Now at stake, that virginal soul;
broken and crush'd to the ground
doubtful to rise as ever before.
Worn out this poor weary soul;
helpless, dejected and confused,
fear'd the worst and awaiting nothing,
Arise and search the giver of life,
seek the peace that he lavishes,
renew, stand in a way different.
Whatever, confident and hold to Him,
that I may live with glory in Him.

84. Tears Shed…

The gentle eyes that twinkle
the dark eyes that shine
the misty eyes that feel
the sleepy eyes that open wide,
could not bear that sight
which moves the inmost heart,
Like the river that flows endlessly,
without barriers it runs down;
just that my tears too gushes
without break it rushes down,
that sight that tore my mind,
that view that stole my thought
those words that made my moment,
that life that changed my mission
that moment I will live and relive;
'I am for your alone', just you.

85. The Man

The journey ahead came to a still
crossroad and dilemma was on the way,
decided to stop and give a quit;
surrender and walk away, I stand.
Hark! the angel of life visited me
a man simple, gentle and giant mind,
listened, guided and showed the way:
the sorrow and of my journey travell'd.
Deep within him was the joy he live,
satisfaction and fulfilment was his life
the smile given, the pain shared,
with the people he chose to serve.
I stumble, fall and committed blunder,
yet I resolved to rise from my weakness
from the hope and inspiration I received
just from the man-angel I know.
I rise realis'd down but not out,
watch me again as I journey along
to the untrodden path of humanity
from the eternal abode of Angels.
Hail! my guide, my mentor,
heaven awaits and opens to receive you,
the man who open heaven's door on earth,
rest in glory, till we join you.

86. Sleep, Blow Thee…

Awake and start off with a sigh
Heavy gloom dragg'd to start anew
Half-awake yet forced to begin
a new day with an old mechanism.
Sleep, I bow to thee, thou enriched,
rest ever on and forget worries.
Arise to rush and renew the mess
you teach life's lesson, less we realise
that we rise to start afresh with zeal
in His service and to serve humanity.

87. Missing Agony

The lonely soul craze for thee, dear;
I can feel in my bosom; thee
the journey set to begin is tested,
shaken bruised and love hurt.
The noble soul I chase to tell you
but shame and silence my soul;
the gentle, noble and cute soul dance
to be just for me, my angel.
She waits my return to her soul,
determined to mine she vowed:
Marry me, I am yours forever
to dance together in the joy of heaven.

88. My friend

Oh! dear friend, you are the only one who
comes to my life and leaves an impact,
as a good friend, come what may,
our friendship will endure forever,
I'll always treat you well by and by,
though out of my sight you are,
but very much in my heart and mind.
As a true friend and tust'd one,
with care and understanding we travel on,
to walk the journey of untrodden destiny,
you are thus, a best friend of mine.

89. True Friendship

True friends are treasures to find,
Hard to leave and let go if found.
True friendship is precious like a gem,
And like a reborn to new life.
True friends share secrets, joys and sorrows,
Tears and laughter together in life's destiny.
True friendship will bloom and endure on,
Spread sweet fragrance in life's garden.
In love and trust the friendship drives,
In all the seasons of my beautiful life.

90. True Love

Life and love was simple, feeling so easy,
not bothering about love, it was a game
never knew true love was eternal, forever.
Love changed my life and strongly it hit,
broken and melted and tears are the proof.
Past became memories, your voice and smile,
now hard to relive, cos' the sting of separation.
Time reckons the heart; life has to march on,
to the untrodden path of destiny with hope,
with life as my true love, never to betray again.